POETRY THROUGH FRESH EYES

ELLIS UNCHAINED

Work of Unchained Wisdom ©2020

Introduction

New perspective, new collection. Opening my eyes fully to the world around us, enabling me to see that love and compassion is paramount to moving our lives into a more positive direction. To this end, the evil need to be highlighted to allow the good to shine through.

I'd like to dedicate this collection to strength and love for everyone.

X

Chapter One:

SHINING IN THE DARK

Delivery of Angels

A shooting star, moves slowly into my peripheral,
burning exuding ruby rays, I blink.
The day grey, your light embraces my skin, gives me
a complexion of pink, I blush and sink.

I sink into your cobalt iris, drowning, the aura of you
recharged me, the heart starts to roll.
Only fifteen the OCD becomes a dream, overthinking
of love, my time to let in another soul.

Your strength exuded the nourishment I needed; my
front was bleeding, you set me free.
In this segment of history, I found my Bonnie, people
can change, an Eleanor I now see.

The roar projected turned to passion, skills obtained
to end life, converted to security,
For my guiding angel, and beautiful offspring, now a
realm of peace and serenity.

Fear of loss degenerated, a boulder became a grain,
making room for the essence of life.
Unconditional love, My Wife.

Fellowship

Concepts of life, parallel with time, only one created
divine.
The other man made, restricting precious minds.
Serpents coil and tighten, paradigms become
irrelevant,
Yearning, it is perpetual love, I adhere.

Peace, the flint for hearts fire, burning for
togetherness.
Resilience in abundance, for all the animal kingdom,
The eagle's noble waltz, eyes beckon freedom,
Ferocious the spirit, kind with soft toughness.

Water flow becomes ice cold, it slows as beauty
forms.
Bonds of millions bind together, inventing security.

In the warmth, she generates power, filling great catacombs,
Cleansing earth's crust from decaying lost souls.
Black and white, good and evil, use different tools.
On the other hand, available to all.
Exceptions of one,
Compassion.
Consume before it falls.

Had to Stop!

Hello, I am Open mind,
I always thought it was, an open mind.
One day I realised it was, a closed mind.
Holy smokes, the door was huge… mind,
Here' a little story from behind the doors mind.

I once judged as I disliked being judged, crazy mind.
Here is a list provided of my thoughts,
That I thought, were mine.

I love this country… I will die for it.
British I am, proud, get the immigrants out.
I am not eating that veg, I ay Buggs Bunny .
Those lefty benders destroy my soul.
That fellow drinks way too much.
Make some money useless, oxygen thief.
It's the Muslims, send them all home!
That Farage is a racist, but his views are clear.
I'm not a racist, but…
I guess I'll join the Infantry, Great Idea!

Once I overdosed on news, spewed up my guts.

Propaganda everywhere, up the walls, looks like fudge.
The minds door burst open!
The thoughts became clear.

Judgement burns in many ways.
So… Just… Stop!

The Light Nurse For Broken Souls

Speckle frog, when I first saw you, darkness had began to consume my thoughts,
The heron was me.
Unfortunately, I was just a boy, disguised as a grown up, fighting in pubs with grown men,
Theoretically they too, were only children of the misery sea.
The beast inside, my speckle smacked the on the nose, to keep the wildling,
From breaking free.
Your picturesque book cover, what first attracted me, pollen from the orchard,
From flower to the bee.
When I read the book, although I couldn't really read, jumbled words showed me,
Your bravery and kindness, true love, I now feel.
You minded your siblings at a tender age, your autopilot for preserving life, I was amazed.
You then chose to do the same for me.
I struggled, my self-worth surfaced for only you, child minding, from one to me.
Now for our own children, I'll repay, now be free!

The oblivion in my mind, chaotic thoughts of death
and retribution, your enveloping mist,
Soothed me, selfish to think you were only sent for
me.
I don't kneel for any entity, though for you I would
bow, on all fours so you can sit on my back,
I'd crawl this earth for your comfort, you are sublime.
My back has broken many times, bones strengthen
and knit, in patience and time.
Now I can lift the many, no need to pay a dime.
My angel, our sweet Jadey, sent from the valleys. You
pieced my fragments together,
from ten thousand directions.
A master puzzle, you completed, just in time.

Middle Ground

Tumbling sound rebounds, on every type of ground,
so many can be found.
The battle ground, filled with emotion, feelings
profound.
Lives taken, as life goes on.

Excitement emits from children playing, innocent
minds acting out life.
The playground filled with positive vibes; thoughts
become bound.
Life creating, as life goes on.

Burrowing matter fixated on a goal, churning up the
dead, new existence evolves.
The underground and its toxicity, the earth worm will
clean in time.

Life sustaining, a must for life to go on.

Altogether, from old to young, the worms under foot,
invigorating from the vibrations.
The fairground everyone's sharing, a common feeling,
happiness.
The show, life certainly goes on.

Sonnet Uno: Poppies from the Valleys

Poppy heads full of life, seeds made of dreams,
Diversity of hue vortex one's mind.
Grow in my heart, your roots run through my
streams,
Water's flow never ends as you are kind.
A quilt of pure magnificence you knit,
Face of many angels, warmth you reside.
My core candles before you, were unlit.
Flower of flowers you always provide.
You will always grow in my garden soul,
Perpetual life you provide the world.
Shattered petals scattered hearts; you make whole.
If you are walked upon, more seeds, be hurled.
Whilst the earth's crust exists, life comes and goes.
Whilst red runs through you, I'll attend the shows.

Sonnet Dos: Eternal

Riptides of allure, currents drag the heart,
Pleasure of your presence brings waves of joy.
Crazy for you, die for you, when apart,
Germanic journeys led to my deploy.
Thoughts I'd always return dead or alive.

Survive a must, you're a ghost without touch,
It's your soft touch that makes the spirit thrive.
Book of life will go on in time, as such.
Put together our moat flowing forever,
Never-ending battles together, win all.
Love our molten shield, tactics so clever.
Me and you together standing so tall.
The world spins and rotates as the cells bond.
Live, let be, swim in the majestic pond.

Legends Germinate From Dirt

The man, the myth, the legend, his philosophy spilled
out on paper, you can pull thousands of quotes, to
help rebalance earth.

Some have investigated William, to end of nowhere to
be seen, some argue he is a collective, pay no mind,
witness the wisdom's birth.

To me I would of never have envisaged only a year
ago, reading such magical words to change my own
thought flow, and worth.

A man who's upbringing was from a glove maker,
schooled in a school for the working class,
Keep his spirit alive, no need for rebirth.

A quote of Shakespeare sticks in my head, in having
much torments us with defect.
Helping words in disguise, documented before his
death.

Inspiration from a man who generated resistance because of his natural talent, I will sing his name from the roof tops, until my last breath.

Perpetual Balance and Love

A magical Struggle of a day, of a different sort,
whispers from my heart, be kind to yourself,
Be humane, the growth will never dissipate.
My gauntlet of fortitude, I choose to pass by the
morning exercise and meditation to witness,
The evolution from the normal day to day.
Exactly eight in the evening, the routine nearly slips,
from the strength, begin, arms reach up, lightning
strikes, energy in array.
The vessel of earth, shakes, the hearts beat stays in
rhythm, perpendicular with heavenly skies, I leave
the plain for a moment, spirits, many a rainbow dance
before my eyes.
Introspection begins, it starts uneasy, joints exuding
pain from the day's occurrences, balance within melts
the pang away.
Tranquility achieved, love now spilling from eyes, it
can't stop, it's in abundance, share it with kin or
project to anyone with thoughts, they are in your
heart.
Feel being elated, sit on the ground, connect with
hydrogen and carbon bound planet, nature will not
steal the energy, it will collaborate.
Peridot orbs illuminate the joining stars, descended to
join the manifestation of power that we all possess,
when the mind has opened.

Sitting in the moisture, unprecedented number of
lives, the grass, true innocents gather at once,
the birds, the insects, true purity of life.
Today's novel reminds me, woke consciousness
should spread balance and love, bring like-minded
people together, demonic interference will run.

Happy

The motion of life's notions, an obstacle, one life of a
billion ego's, projected from the same oculus. Events,
pantomimes, stories, whatever we choose, there will
be a beginning, a middle, but never an ending.

Care is fair, the most important way, create and share,
caring devours hate and differences.
It moulds divides into multiplication, transmits
smiles, retunes feelings and manufactures joy for
sending.

They made the world so hard, Robert. M kept on
fighting, the battle has no need for violence or raining
judgment, project happiness and calm, the powers
that be would show true colours, they would stop
pretending.

The heart is the base of everything, so create whatever
feelings you're thinking, be mindful and present, let
love shine through, the brain is only for projecting.

Empathic Weld

Opening of energy channels, of aqueducts flowing thoughts, of not yourself, but all.

Eyes of Hawk's see pray from miles away, as our hearts view human concern.

If we don't see pain, a band aid required for the main conscious, the world is all our concern.

We are born empathic, bound by truth and kindness, passion crumbled by society,
 a dustpan collects all.

Systematically we compete, our main spirit depletes, emancipation from modern temptation, releases power from the demons in our ear.

Today is the most important, today not tomorrow, nor yesterday. Perennial forbearance will cascade.

Humans are plants, walking the earth, plants are humans, buried in the earth, animals of the kingdom are no different, for sure.

Respect, a moisturiser, would outsell loreal or tilbury's magic serum, don't waste your time,
 clogging your pores.

Speculation tests one's patience, release from this notion, perplexed by old ghosts, who you gonna call? Each other.

Walking through life forward, is a must, but we should face backwards to see the inherited light, we all traveled from.

Romance is dead, no way! I'll sway and dance, in the rain of love, porn and EastEnders, speak no truths.

If a man falls to his knees, press your hearts together, wrap him tight and levitate to heights, we all deserve.

When a lady feels ugly, project and connect, to the beauty they can't see, the light of souls, all have the same glow.

Children decoupled from parents, teach them not to judge, Mother nature showers perpetual love.

Tracy chapman's revolution sounds like a whisper, let's start shouting it and stick together, a gorilla glue manifestation.

Compassion, Kindness and Love.

In need, anytime

Efforts cause an effect, the ripple on the lake makes it to the other side.
Care and compassion, the stone that created the movement, the lakebed they reside.
Stones will stop being thrown; they are there for whom ever would like.
You know where to find them, they never hide.

Mature Cheddar

When young, looking past parents, to see the Grand.
The warmth of the withering touch made me stand,
Perplexed by the strength at hand.

Hard as John Wayne, as gentle as trifle, Sunday
afternoon.
The wisdom you possess, takes me to the moon,
If only the youth could be made, from where you
came.

Events from history, with our eyes, we see no
vulnerability.
Lived through wars, strikes and adversity.
If your label has an error, tell them, I'm ok, strong
forever!
Frequency of love, wave lengths uncontrolled, no toll.
Tune into HOPE, togetherness the lock.
BBC, not the Key.

Strength, in all, to see.

We love our Oldies.

The Do Ron

The old man, the taxi man, the café breakfast cook on
a Saturday morning.
The scent of bacon, the alarm clock, energy for the
days adventure.

Off to the tip on a scorching summers day, it smelt like…
Regardless of the odor, I was with a true best friend.

Road trips to talybont, I smell the sea from hundreds of miles away.
The scent reminds me of how great a man you are.

Travelling back in the middle of your break from work, to work only to return.
You did all in your power and more, to keep a whole family a float.

My number one activity, rummaging for what seemed hours at the car boot.
I was as excited as you felt, with your first sip of cold bitter.

I cherish the days we laughed and tittered at all your wonderous tales.
With all this compassion I learnt not to be a quitter.

The morals I gained as a dustbin lid, doused the flame you attempted to ignite.
Now my mind is clear, it's your teaching that remains.

I acknowledge I was a pain in the arse, thank you for all you've done.
Thursdays, Saturdays and Sundays were my light in the dark.

A Father of all Fathers, a man who never let me down.
You'd do anything for anyone, above and beyond.

An inspiration, a sanctuary, it's time to settle down, don't worry anymore.
Whatever happens in time, remember the world keeps going around.

I love you and if anyone can do it, the do Ron can!

Otherworldly Theft

Day evolves to night, a child's eyes held tight.
Tremors from the cerebellum,
Through the kaleidoscope with smite.

The monkey swinging humpty dumpty,
Avoiding the shadow in the corner,
Peace welcome instead of fear.

Waving to waxing, obstacles and objecting.
The ape, the raven blanket, bring comfort,
What core values are they detecting.

The pressure, the rope of the animation,
Segments increase, thoughts decrease,
The reversal of emancipation.

Great forest matures when left unappeased.
The kaleidoscope, the monkey, the shadows,
They all disappeared.

Battle commences through glass, with the lost.
Victorious Velvet cut from the same cloth,
Who won, only the ghost.

Hidden warriors, combat in vain,
the battle rages on now, through sand,
Destruction in hand, heart searing in pain.
Onyx tumbling into black, the kaleidoscope returns,
Bringing souls to their knees, except one.
They Wail, revolt, refusing to be ceased.

A welcoming sight, it has been too long,
The monkey and the shadow are heard.
The whole spectrum at last returns.

Thirteen Miles Beyond

Pursuing the furnace in the heavens, searing lapis
lazuli, tinting with carmine.
Clouds dissipate with unconscious emotions they slip
away, the feeling divine.

Antithesis in choice, energies pull the other way, I do
not resist, the universe at play.
The bun settles in the kiln for sable to return, I keep
moving my spirit shines as day.

Tree's now settle from the dance of day, resting,
shining from the light it retains,
Movements becomes ghostly, the minds keep stays
focused on beauty it maintains.

The journey so far as presented a fox, it stops the emerald glow from her eyes fills mine,
The lofty bats mesmerize as they dance, the echolocation to my ears, I see through my time.

From the beginning there was light now we are in the dark, balance sails to mind.

A journey is a journey. Enchanted by mother's shadow.

Thirteen miles beyond.

I'm still home.

Rightful Queens

You are amazing, life within life, two hearts in sync, the great symphony.
A beginningless novel, oppressed, this chapter is yours.
Together we are equal, love, respect and equality we adore.

You were once openly worshiped, cremation, forced by holy service.
I adore you openly, you make balance, strength and care,
Gift them to the physical, to protect universal life.

The beauty I see in all of you, even under the morning paint.

I will never understand, why you cover the angel's
face.
We love you, wipe those thoughts away.

You are our Frigg, our Aphrodite, our Athena,
Goddesses I say.

Worlds Apart, Tied by Heart

Contemplation of emancipation, I am free but
trapped, as the creature of the safari, until they
stumble upon the fence.

Dictators, manipulators, corporations selling dreams,
my thoughts are past the clouds now, I think I've lost
the receipt.

Effigies of tribe's men, the magicians and doctors of
the forest, a way for many years untouched, I'd join
you on a whim.

My balance is of difficulty, amongst the man moulded
ridges, they are unpredictable, chaotic, problematic,
and steep.

My Journey has halted, the reason I see, a brick wall,
take it down, brick by brick or maybe I'll go around,
though I cannot see the edge.

Concrete jungles that surround us, crushing like the
pressure of the ocean, forcing life from our bodies,
then diluted into sea.

A red kite in spirit, the pins are emerging from the down, nearly time to spread those wings and truly start to exist.

Warble and Proceed to Move

Singing as the tiny bird is heard, a chirp of a verse,
Difference is none from the onyx bird.
The crow's bellowing is heard.

Sounds born are bound to be caught by the receiver.
Journeys through molecules, no reverse,
Creations are of no concern.

Singing releases emotion notes bouncing off bones,
Jump, dance, waltz, be free, go loco.
Please magical traditions reform.

Sound, can you hear it? Close your eyes, you feel it,
Always be ready to perform fun and joy,
Use little effort to conform.

Chapter Two:

SHADOWING THE LIGHT

The Cave

Allegory of the cave, a theory from Plato, to me it's
factual, my reasoning,
The proof showers us, as soon as we leave.
Real sun light burns the iris, the light of TV reddens
them, burns within.
Grit your teeth, don't go back inside, the eyes adjust
eventually.
The puppet shadows of today, imprinted on our
visual cortex, stain like bleach.
Brexit, virus, racism and, divide, divide, divide.
Beautiful people, chained to the wall, I see the
puppeteer coming, history repeats itself.
They're coming with recycled puppets, war, war, war.
The shackles to the brick wall of pink Floyd are very
loose, stand up turn away.
Walk the steps. Only this way it will fall.
If you're comfortable in the gloom of the cave, be
mindful of those who chose to leave.
Is that possible? Maybe it's an egocentric puppet,
we've already been shown.
Over and over and over and over again!

Fading Injustice

The British settle in Australia in 1788, how is this to settle, when aborigines were unsettled.
Captain Phillip led boats of convicts who slowly died.
Phillip quotes, there will be no slavery, the prisoners they had taken, some for petty crimes,
Now working for food and what else? Today we call them... slaves.
Photographic evidence portrays a British family, head of the house wielding a whip, surrounded by aboriginal people, caged pigeons waiting for crumbs.
This devilish behavior moves into 1870, British officers accepting so called luxuries of India, being fanned, having pedicures, by you guessed it, slaves.
The British, the evil empire, skip it's history to 1952, native courts of Sudan, traditions of years and years, now a pompous district commissioner judging their crimes.
The British weren't pioneers of abolishing slavery, they modernised, to camouflage the horrific actions, which continue today.
Poor Elizabeth's coronation in 1953, now a puppet with the blood of Mary and George running through her veins, purpose and reasons for war drastically changed.
History they let us see, shows that we've always been slaves, unfortunately some treated more like dogs, a geographical lottery in ways.
If you're in debt, work ungodly hours and pay tax of every kind, perhaps this is why we don't notice the more unfortunate ones, because we are all technically enslaved.

The rulers of the world have always created turds, for the poor, now they have become masters of concealment, with glitter and sprinkles. They cannot polish a turd.
Inspect the Georgian calendar, see how many days we celebrate world suffering, at the hands of those whose blood still reigns today.
A stealthy leap backwards for mankind, hip, hip, hooray, so the memories fade away.

Dangerous Games!

Here we go again, piling misery, creating divides through terror and pain,
Chaos out the gates of oblivion, a perpetual breeze, does it ever end?
The kingpins you follow freely, surging to new levels by virtue of personal gains.
They sit demonic, feeding and fattening, on the energy you pay.
Are we forgetting the last campaign, maximum fear, now proves lame?
Proof is in the blood pudding, no one genuinely cares.
Operation Julius Caesar, divide and conquer, simple while masses run insane.
Brothers and sisters, you are playing into their hands.
I'm tired and bored of repeating, history repeats itself, it's time for new campaigns.
Throughout history we fight for them, now each other for the same!
The new I-spy, I mean eye phone, stick it in your orifice, as the world divides and children starve!

For what? Cash, acceptance, a career… oh my, all that
work and then we die!
Remember the extraordinary number of deaths from
playing these games,
Please remember, we all bleed the same.
Black, white and anything in between, our heart's
beat in rhythm,
At the moment to the tune of misery and pain.
A new tune to waltz to, equalness and love, this does
not make you into those heroes,
Portrayed on the screen, sitting pretty while your
mind loses control.

Base Jumping Without a Parachute

The mobile phone, the new TV, the ultimate media
administration device.
Social media, the health crumbler, the chains, the
ultimate manipulator.
Keyboard warriors, dopamine chasers and
dramatising hyenas.
Thoughts of a new kind, pulverising the mind from
pre world wars.
Apps for everything, from banking to finding a
partner, we don't live in the world,
We live in a screen, for all to be seen, do we see
anymore?
You want a job or a career, or to only socialise? Get a
phone, it's all A.I.
Misinterpreted messages; true emotion gone!
The tablet is our babysitter, kids' mental health in
tatters, on par with the adults.

We are all at it, the world has forgot about snap, a social game.
Ads after ads, in game purchasing, the scrolling causes fatigue, need energy?
It reads your mind; up pops just eat.
Corporations don't care, we are cannon fodder, fired to the doctors to be prescribed,
Antidepressants and moisturising solution for the eyes.
Unfortunately, this is now life, socialising in person, is talking to the camera,
Or the top of a head, while eyes gaze at the phone.
Try your best with the utmost courage, to put the damn thing down,
It is distracting us from way too much.
NHS sell off, loss of human rights, child trafficking, corruption, compassion,
Real kindness, genocide, and our dreams.

Peculiar Ways

Class divides are created with only bad intentions in mind.
A pecking order to keep order, no wonder true good loses its mind.
Why do famous figures fight for social injustice, while they sit in luxury homes?
Empty bedrooms, full fridges while other humans' roofs are the sky.
Fame and control the lubrication, money is the goal, morals buried for a slice of the trillion-dollar pie, now further away from the original pastry.

Networking can be wondrous, a net to cover all, when true colours prevail.
The fray hangs the people below, pretentious, ostentatious, by products of the shit show.
The classes dividing masses are distorted by cash is king, most forget it's also the root of all evil, What does that say about the one percent of the world?
Power, fame, and fortune are the tools of a fool.

Careers for Cowpat

Boris Johnson and all your predecessors, whether blue or red have lied, there is nowhere to hide.
The tales you've spun on Brexit and many other subjects, have been printed on time.
Lying snakes who only care for gain, are always surrounded by entities, playing the same game, the so-called experts who perverse the facts, to increase their worth and gain. They all think the same.
Why should good, hard-working people struggle, while you let loose in your ungodly private parties and meetings, whilst pushing oppression, how do they believe your tales?
Scientists who concoct facts, while we are never shown the proof, boost investments made by prominent figures, who is invested in face masks, a flow of liquidity I wonder, face masks for sale!
It's fake news if not from your bull covered mouth, or your puppets, that's a bit rich for the pallet, from a liar with the media in a choke hold.
Packs of foul entitled politicians; I hope the world awakes to your shackles of control, and pays no mind to you bunch of pointless lying arseholes.

The Periodic Shake-Up

What a load of croc shit, to prepare us for a great
reset,
We haven't been sick with fever, but with fear.
No more cash will soon be on us, our every move will
be tagged,
As the cows from the heard, through their ear.
Cattle we are to the ones who cause animosity,
They are the greatest threat here.
The only difference I see between us and cattle,
The cows stick together.
Let us not forget we all have warriors deep inside,
The media, the subliminal, have our warriors in a
cage.
We do not have anything to fear,
In the end, we all die.
It's not screens and masks that have kept us safe,
It's a natural animal instinct to survive.
I'll wear a mask and play along sometimes,
As I respect everyone's views
To that end, love and be kind,
And one last thing, the royal family is useless and
fudge BBC news.

Propaganda

Philosophy is dying, critical thinking from the
philosopher does not create value.
It strips power from the powerful.
One great philosopher unfairly tried, came from the
bottom, joined wars,

For whom he ceased to believe, yet still they succeed.
If you believe google's skewwhiff take on history,
from those that keep us inline,
Naive daydream, springs to mind.
Astrology being driven to extinction, so we don't
think past our tiny solar system,
And question the bull of today.
Ironically, another philosopher, a cosmological
genius, Giordano Bruno, excited, enlightened,
Rushed to tell Clement the VIII's Henchmen the
news.
Why did they banish and torture him, try to make
him repent his beliefs and theories?
Now they teach what he was writing, and they
watched him burn.
The corporation who murdered and spread lies,
travelled the world, forcing their ways.
We believed them and still they exist today.
Study from books and material that are not
mainstream, investigate, compare both sides,
Validate your point of view, don't allow half-truths to
do it for you.
Drink a glass of purified water, stop choking on the
partisan, drench the mouth,
Stop spitting feathers, nonsense dries it out.
The greats, trying to set minds free, or possibly just
bring balance.
Now there is more bad than good, demonic
interference.
The bad guys still running this show, who taught you
how to be, with work and single-minded education,
They shackle, while breathing hell fire into our souls.

Reincarnation of Jesus, Lao Tzu, Buddha, Samson,
Moses and Socrates, would be a lot to hold.
Religions divided these, I believe they would have
been best buddies.
They sent messages of love and freedom, to assimilate
with the universe,
Now they are used as tools, in sadistic control
methods.
As so well said by Mr Marley,
How long shall they kill our prophets, of love, peace
and freedom?

Dehumanization Nation

The human race, an odd bunch, falling off a cliff face,
tiny pebbles join more, gaining momentum, to the
bottom, tumbling past boulders stubbornly in place.
A race from the Olympics, the gold medal at the
bottom. Gold that was dug from the earth by slaved
workers, jewelry on a wrist or penetrated through a
face.
The human race, swirling like the Tasmanian devil,
screaming and hissing at everyone that moves, or just
passes by, frantically looking for food, as we
rummage through Primark hungry for new clothes.
The taste of the food is an acquired one, becoming
accustomed to the sweet sweat of children who
delicately sewed them, a disgrace.

The human race, soar like the Canadian goose, across countries to new destinations, pumping fuel that's sucked from the earth, it was there for a reason, not for a fool landing in a country. It's so cheap, pay no mind to the beggars in the markets though, my conscience is clear, not really though, do we really care, clear it's a no.

The human race loves food like Augustus Gloop loved cake, overindulging, the belly takes over, watch teen titans, Belly bro's. The Labrador will just swallow whole like a pelican, this is all they know, but we, know better. Food standards taking a dive, why worry? We've been eating crap forever. No worries, keep popping medication, they now deliver on the go.

The human race, ruled by emotions, intertwined with money, a deadly concoction. An overdose of communism, disguised as democracy, like zombies consuming brains for survival. Just consume your five a day and meditate, restore your energy and clear the excrement away. Communism has poisoned our way, it's getting thicker in our veins, put down the spy phones today.

The human race, can you hear me, Enrique, I'm giving in, no chance! My life has only just begun, to move in directions, that make me feel so good. Free from the constraints of today, mental health, violence, judgment, and hate, I gave it all the middle finger for the last time, as I'm trying not to swear. Like the magpie, trying not to be an ass, battle on, it can be grey.

Love everyone, even if they can't love back. Be aware, good people, we were all born with the light, even if you think you're good, your actions may still not be right.

Have You Got A Conscience!

Hello Western society. Have you got a conscience? Let us delve into the question, if you melt easily, sit in the freezer because this is going to get toasty.
Child slavery is the base, the driving force, bringing your phones to life and your fancy jewellery, while kids are whipped to work for nothing, but fear.
Western society how do you sleep, easy clutching devices and self-pity. We believe we lived through hell, try fitting in shoes of the child servile concubine.
Cobalt, lithium, gold, and silver make nearly all our pointless gadgets, that turn us into selfish zombies, while children are whipped raped, and bombed on a daily basis.
They get nothing, only torture and still make time to smile unlike us pathetic creatures, if you do not like it, go cry a river and go to the doctors.
A long absence from living in society, will boggle your brains, upon on return, you see western society are no longer human, auto-bots we have become.
Keep on pushing for nothing, causes that have no point or only for fame and financial return. This will only fuel the fire, so kids continue to burn!
Get a fudging grip, nation of closet hypocrites, find that real conscience, before there is no return. If this has made you butt hurt, do not comfort eat chocolate!

Cadbury's have left their fair-trade deal, to join another one, now thousands are not getting paid, that means all the kids slaving, have done it for double nothing. What a damn shame.
As if you give a shit! As you will pay the driving force and for a million, you would do the same.

Sacrificial Joy, Oh Well!

The masses are starting to smell the coffee, too late.
Loved him for a few weeks by the late coffee smellers.
Too late the coffee shop is closing.
Hopefully, you'll remember those, who put it under your nose,
In the early stages, instead of scaring them away with zombie mentality.
Oh well maybe next time.
Fear will now be turned against you, as with the none threat of Muslims.
Like the threat of Iraq, now we keep bombing.
Oh well, humans are sacrificial, like human emotions!
Oh well, we seem to enjoy it!

Tinted Windows

A bed of nails, the pinnacle of uncomfortable, lying punctured and bruised as thoughts of investigating the truth, no one believes, until the anger sets in.
Ear infections are spread by ludicrous messages entering the canal, sending the neurons into fits within the brain, do you feel that tightness again.

That dumb looking mother fudger, spreading nonsense about the epidemic, from behind his tiny desk, pushing for a hasty sell off of the NHS.

Whilst the decoy is in place, he's pushing for the final quarter to be flogged, while the working-class fight like silly children, the act of push and pull.

Health insurance will be a must if you like to pop them pills, universal credits is a wage now, so you'll have to pay, be careful and save.

4th of July, Independence Day, ironically for the UK, the day we can go back to the pub and destroy our liver day. America's last laugh day.

I quoted several months ago, be aware of the monetary system, they need more oldies to go, so we can get rid of the paper they fought for.

Australia's contactless payment, now at two hundred dollars, the UK's is slowly creeping up, shops shouting, we do not accept your paper money.

The end of the right to a jury trial has been suggested, massive cuts to the judicial system, human rights you may be losing, is Hunger games a true story?

Twenty Indian soldiers killed, in a fist fight with the Chinese at the border, Indian military have allowed weapons again, china is setting up.

While the epidemic continues, distraction from all above and much more, the damage has been done, while the tinted protective screens have been installed.

While these times have been a misery for most, the slippery sadistic serpents have been capitalising, from the depths of hell.

The con men are not only at the top, they walk amongst normal ladies and men, beware good people, Make up your own minds.
Don't get left behind, actually do, it's quite fun, when you don't trust a word anyone on the TV says, they are just puppets, with a power-hungry hand shoved up their bum.

Unsaintly

The innocent, the eighth, close friends with the explorer, not Dora, thankfully.
The innocent funds his first expeditions, creating millions of jobs, Slavery.
Doorways to heavenly destruction, paving way to replace free tribes.
The want to absorb more and more power, the riches before his eyes.
Commodities are king, the decoy, silly faces stamped on pressed trees.
This made his name, a maritime executioner, excuse me, explorer.
Now, many souls delivered or bound in chains, still today.
October, we celebrate!
Instead investigate and gaze at what Da Vinci says!

The Judicial Officer

Earth established in the way's logical endless life, governments entrench, trenches in the essence, for the chiefs we do not see!
Creatures who brush off this evil, success it blinds.

Do not judge anybody, archon contracts already
signed.
Unfortunately, the details never printed in braille.
The crashers enter through forex,
Rallying aspirers, to slash and divide.
So demons in existence, shapeshift, lurk, and hide.
Judging, the product of society, today's sought-after
entertainment.
Feel the misery, as the soul quivers insane.
Relief through the judge, to spread your pain.
This is not the way!
Sure hope the sun exuberates, to dry the judgment
rein.

You Turn

We want change for justice, we want peace.
We need a world of chaos, converted to serene.
A goal unachievable, because the world's king,
Is currency and personal endeavor.
You may fathom your deeds to be good,
How much do you care when it's payday?
This doesn't make you bad, just blind.
Entities that obliterated the Saxons, the same
for the Indians, then moved in for the Africans.
If your worries are for pennies or millions, divided
into
what you like, subconsciously, you've already joined
them.
Charities and organisations vow to make change.
While the CEO's sit in mansions. Children in need,
raised over

One billion since inception, why are children still starving?
Cheese and onion, salt and vinegar, all different flavours.
Hate, racism, and judgement, all made from potatoes.
It's a mental issue, if we all downed tools for a few days,
We would see, who really needed whom!
Unfortunately, it's digits in our bank accounts,
That defines the world.
While beloved is wealth, don't expect change.

Life Grater

Time of time, time we pay, something highly valued today.
Time is worth nothing if we cannot retain.
Instead we sell it on, like the water companies sell us rain!
Crying is nothing to be ashamed of, even if, crying in vein.
Love, peace, and tranquility creates longevity, to regain your time.
Cry in a sea of calm, this will ease the pain.
Chasing fame, or wealth is destination lost.
When you have it, the life grater will remove it.
Not the money or the fame, it's your sanity they claim!

Waste

Wow, it has barely been a week, Macy D's trash already painting the streets, reversal I see.

The litter starts to pile once again, chippie wrappers
fly on by, as do our dreams.
Economy tit for tat, here you go one hundred billion,
the pound has a split, it is starting to sink.
We will pay it back with liquidity, so puppeteers do
not scrape their hull.
Co co crazy coherent puppets, here is the cliff, please
do not jump!
Scared of Covid-19, what about the carcinogenic food,
pollution and all the above.
Under full control, countries are accidentally invading
others, while assuring it was a mistake.
The wool has grown to our eyes now, the Chinese
and Indians are having a brawl, I smell war.
The masses are drooling over retail, all I need is a hug
and freedom from a system mug.
Let me be and live in the woods.

The Dogs Spoils of War

Belly down in the sand, the warmth penetrates my
Ubac,
Strangely Cool from the clear open sky, the Stars so
beautiful, no time to gaze.
A klick beyond, snaps, and cracks, like whips
breaking atoms, ring out.
A vision through night vision, bullets glow emerald, a
sight to behold.
Our safety, a claymore, little less than a hundred
yards, barbwire and 2 rifles we guard.
Trained for what seemed a lifetime for slaughter, my
kill switch now engaged.

Patrolling on foot in searing terrain, the core of the universe melts us,
Moistening rocks from sweat of our souls, noise pollution from the warriors' growl.
I kneel by a stream, water, a pleasant sight to see, my awakening starts to evolve.
A child bounds up to me, a cheeky little fellow, brings some joy, thank you little friend.
I gave him a M16 muzzle cover, he was delighted and stuck it on my friends SA80,
It was stuck, he was elated, we laughed as my buddy panics trying to remove.
Language barriers no problem for me, it's the connection of souls.

Now I see the rabbit hole, I start the descent, stopped by a call, I.E.D on a friendly call sign.
A decision from a so-called leader, five of us now left alone, to face the innocent enemy,
Thankfully, they never arrived, probably something to do with the, not so equal force flying in the sky.

Washing day is upon me, I need some fresh clothes, two washing machines between a battalion,
I'll just use my hands and a bowl, a sickening boom shaking my core and shivering my soul.
Now an American in pieces, the golden hour, I hope he survived,
Now for honor we gift the afghani's head, back to the brother in a sharps box, I was horrified.

Time has slowed hugely, the heat beginning to cool, or are we becoming climatised to the scorch.

The death becomes no bother, to this end another brother takes a round to the head.
The same section goes again, another headshot from miles away.
A human sacrifice to flush the mercenary out, we succeed, another family without a son.

The morale in lashkar Gah was nonexistent, chatter between friends almost gone. If we had problems, Ask the Fish, he'll know, full of kindness and wisdom, one man with rank I truly loved.
Taken away from us, his wife, and children, I cry flooding tears, I can only think, why?
I cannot take it anymore, all those crimes, deaths, and lies.

Now soldiers being led astray, head shed made it uncomfortable from day one,
The CO had a sadistic way, punishing men in many ways, it all became too much.
He started punishing men for getting unwell, although it was the time of year.
We were briefed about this, but he was too almighty to attend, probably eating cheese and pickle,
With his knob, I mean noble friends.

It was my time for punishment, for not doing as I was told, funnily enough, I was carrying out tasks,
From another order, from another rank, a fool, a mix up, but his tiny gnat balls chocked him.
He saluted and bowed, I told him rip those papers up, I'm appealing, tell the CO I disagree.

It doesn't work like that, we normally take it on the chin, I respond, not me! We will see.
I showed the battalion what he was about, you probably guessed, now I'm the black sheep.

I'm standing for justice and what's right, to help protect the dogs of war and everyone lost.
Even the enemy, so called, I proceed to ask the forbidden question, why are we here?
I was met with resistance, no answer, now all I want is home.

Propaganda and lack of education is what got me there, that's why my medals have been thrown,
The start of a process, to regenerate my gong and soul.

Adios Amigos

This way of living is not for me, I am sorry, I must leave.
This material world of self-pity and anguish, I have attempted to defeat.
The wars, the battles, I've prayed to many gods, on my knees.
As many have blindly knelt, to continue this life of division and low counts of steam.
My Heart once mended by self-care has again began to seep.
What compelled me to fight for people, has lost its meaning, the soul needs resting.
Harsh reality breaks my barrier, as did the infantry, help can only come within.

The life I was being sold, I am not buying, nor am I a salesman.
I'll be here for anyone.
You can find me!
I will be sitting.
Finally, in peace!

Chapter Three:

A CONCOCTION

Where the Hell is Hell!

The dales rolling hills of greenery and wonder for miles and miles.
Cavities and shafts that lead to catacombs, on the surface we look down.
Height fear washes away with the waterfall that cascades the sides.
The power within, strokes the whole body in one motion, the unknown resides.
Within the earth's crust, the soundless sound caresses your ossicle,
A symphony, even Mozart could not replicate, a call to live or decimate.
This new feeling of calm, clears the mind, exploring becomes symbolical.
The urge emerges, go deeper, keep going, against the dark obstacle.
Subterranean realms provide tests of courage and overcoming trepidation.
The gaps become inches; we can do it if the babe can arrive.
Do not go backwards, the unknown is marvellous, resist the temptation,
Discovery is why we are here, the deep so magical, in the depths, the mind thrives.
On the surface, tribulation is alive, down here, calm will set in, we will survive.

Carving My Own

Modern day is the new age, new algorithms.
Magnetic force, complex killings of messianisms.
Move back, stand up, look there's still misogynism.
Paper money I.O.U complex situations, make way for
digital currency.
Paper cash we die for, will be valued at nothing, as
your occupancy.
Pay good vibes, only fund is love, trump the opposite,
Rancid pungency.

Turbulence provided by multimedia, of every variety.
Toughness within, to decompress the anger of society.
Truth, critical thinking for the masses should be
priority.

Bind together no compromise, systems, titles, demise.
Remove the rose tint, see with your own Eyes.
Or keep them on if everything is Hunky-dory.

Just relax, stop shouting about it.
Let them write your story!

Cause the Effect

Daydreams from within the skull projecting,
dissecting another dream,
absorbing nightmares are choice, the widening of the
fissure.

We hear this, we hear that, whilst sitting in silence,
the tainted imagination,
Can leave an adult feeling confused and petulant.

Nerves of the system, fire continuously as the
lightning bug sways the night sky,
This show, a piece of filigree.

Snowballs of negativity, gain momentum and
volume, uncontrollably, before it crashes,
Into the solar plexus, don't forget peace, close the
portcullis.

Old ways dressed up in altered disguises, the acts of
acts can tear hearts away.
Now only connections lost and filched.

The chord that rings now is of mystery, a concoction
of dark and wondrous.
Making waves, creating new strains, a cacophony.

The sun rises as does the moon, on and on, over and
over, in circles and cycles.
Is this our prophecy?

Endowment of Present

The Simplest process, diffusion low energy, material
consumption.
Spreading through matter of life with ease.

Message of today' modern day, tainted by man-made.
Most men never made better for mankind.

Dream' for nations to realise, nature has been compromised.
The currency we pay, mental health in disguise.

Hearts racing, daily flutters, souls quiver and run from demise.
Respiratory rises and falls, our balance left behind.

Eyes closed, we see darkness, chase away notions of that unborn.
Eradicate past and future, let present reform.

Bright clarity my friends.

The one.

Equals be Equals

Master of one's self is the master of a universe.
The lover of one's self joins roads, they traverse.
The lioness is all, let's the alpha think he's the greater.
If she snaps, Mr. lion becomes a master debater.
Females Grow life, they incubate the purest of form.
Males are a seed gun, and most lost nuts, the norm.
Love and care, a great cement, bonds that never crumble.
For peace, war hammers will appear to save life from a tumble.
As an everyday notion, we should be kind to everything.
Animals, insects, plants, girlfriends, boyfriends, wives, and husbands.

Love wasps don't swat, they will pop off, a buzz they
will be singing.
If you do swat, they turn into pricks and that is what
you'll be receiving.

The Human

The wolf pack bind and protect each other, love, and
feed together,
No self-gain, life between them the purest essence.
The wolf full of compassion, will mother a pickney of
a different kind,
This show swells my heart, like riverbanks of April.
The wolf, selects natural leaders, brave, fierce, and
master providers,
Their alpha, the rose's center and his family the
petals.
The wolf to me gives the feeling, that the human is
bottom of the pile,
Tricked into believing we are top, sadly we are
wrong.
The humans fight each other, for self-gain, children
with no parents.
People should bow in shame.
If the delusion of this illusion, controls your everyday,
I suggest,
Being a wolf for rest of your days.

Atomic Bonds, Like it or Not

We are all friends and family, connections are never
ending, whether we like it or not.

Bound together by neutrinos, our make-up identical,
we share the same light, like it or not.
Some poems, some stories, some fiction, some fact, all
made from words, like it or not.
Used as outlets or expressive projecting, all art, I see it
for that.
Hate, selfishness, and judgment, will only harm
yourself.
Friend or Foe, you choose, just don't forget to relax.

Little Wolf Playing Sheep

This is a second poem from my daughter's friend,
about allowing more phone time. My response below:

Untitled

The suffering and pain
You have caused is insane
Do you want lacy to cry
So want me to die
So let her be free
Or I Will eat you knees.

My Response:
Little Wolf Playing Sheep

Children of the world starving clouded in disease.
That's Insane!
Youths in brick houses with food, who complain.
That's Insane!
Government zombies will eat your brains,
That's insane!

That's more likely to happen before you eat my knees,
Insane!
If your third eye doesn't see the bigger picture,
you'll never see past screens.
Your point would have had more punch,
if the mind wasn't reprogrammed by devices!

Illusion of Reality

Reality is a manifestation of images and words and
rules, spoon fed to us, starting around the tender age
of three or four.
We receive moments of joy, when the light bulb
illuminates your thoughts, but fear creeps in, then our
reality slams the door.
When we ponder on a subatomic level, malaise will
settle in your bones, to prompt you back into the cage,
where the gate is always ajar.
When we dream, we have no limits, when awake, this
way of life is pre created, to enunciate the life we are
living, normal has moved too far.
We are nothing but energy, a collection of quark and
perpetual electricity, so why fear the unknown, it's
less scary than our preserved reality.
Diverted from true meaning, the universe chants in
rhythm, revoir, revoir, revoir.

The Dad, Not The Owner.

Panic, possesses my chest seeing the kids in uniforms,
they chose school,
Free choice for the young and old.

With freedom to do as you please, there's great responsibility,
Be warm and kind, not bitter and cold.
Told myself once, they'll grow to adults and build their own roads.
They will never hear the end of my lectures, love and be kind.
Unfold life as you go, my stars, just remember right from wrong,
Have your own philosophy and believe in your heart.
Learn left from right, this is why your Mom…
Destination she never finds.

The Queue

Person behind person, waiting, waiting, and waiting.
Chattering, debating, commiserating.
Everyone moving inch by inch, patience held by a pinch.
A pinch of patience.
They reach the entrance, an opening of magnificence.
The swamp covered in algae, a look ungodly.
Some souls turn, go home and dream of lamentation.
Others swim, self-motivation.
The island, the mean majestic mold, a journey to divergence.
Verdant layers split; the stench is imagination.
Believe your journey is of your thoughts, not of temptation.
The queue, deliberation.

The Concert

The heart at the core pumping in time with thought,
in rhythm with the composer's wave,
Ventricles drive love, infinitely to cells and atoms, for
miles and miles.
Don't let pressure drive us apart.
Joy and anger an epoxy, held together by the
drummer of our own philosophy,
Seeking equilibrium, more consistency, happy should
not be episodic.
Doubts of doubts depart.
Tangled notions played out by the orchestra in the
cranial theater, unwanted pieces of art.
The intonation of the tribulation change one's tune
with instruments of mindfulness.
Caress the strings from the heart.
The drummer, the orchestra, and the composer can be
coaxed to your own concert.

The Symptom Forest

The forest, impossible to be explored, trunks that
interweaved, unrivalled pressure.
Constricting each other, capable of suffocating vines
for pleasure.

The earth, they are born from dry and volatile, no life
within, only the Fraxinella,
Bringing forth fires from hell, smelting life's factual
treasure.

Smoke twists and bellows from the crevices of
entanglement, the heat exudes.

Curly oak, gas plant, your caged in bars of hate and desire, where is the fire?

This mirage I perceive is the prize of a closed mind, I now know what is real.
I lift my somatic arms and crash them on the field of force.

I begin to wail, my mind is already open, a whisper from vibrating energy.
Human form is easily fooled, the physical realm is but a dream.

I close my eyes, disconnect from the matter of science, connect with the matter unknown.
Dark matter it's called, to divert from the thought.

I conjure the dark edge of insanity, an axe to chop I wield, I'll force my way inside.
Please, it whispers, I'll leave you empty, hush, the axe is all you need.

Looking back at my vessel, it convulses as the axe crashes with the barrier,
The forest laughs, your fuel is anger, I realise I'm fighting fire with fire.

I talk within and repeat, to penetrate this iron cloak, this is no task for force.
Something is preventing me, I get knotted as I turn.

The roots of the forest grow from my physical form, embedded into the truth that's born,

The attachment of attachments poisons the mind.

There are so many eyes to see another, one I found I
closed another, relief washes me.
The fingers of the rhizome slip from my soul.

The realisation from relief, the levels of mystery are to
behold, over time,
In good time, I'm going to visit them all.

The battle axe swiftly melts away, I move forward
with grace, collaborating with photons,
Now in the centre, the tree weeps, don't leave, I'm all
you've seen.

Great forest, you've fit your purpose, I have more to
see, burning bush, I created you.
Tree, I did so you, burn your last great fire, peace you
shall now bring.

Black rain of ash now settles to the ground, a colossus
patch of emptiness,
to which I see fit to grow and sing.

Anger, attachments, the chasing of imprisoned souls,
will not be allowed to grow.
The things that weakened me, are now only nutrition
for pure growth.

A sanctuary of balance and love, for all to come and
go, even for a moment of peace.
A glow placed within, come back to recharge at will.

A forest of new untangled, decluttered, a place to leave behind manufactured emotion.
From the material realm, the new forest will take care of them.

Negativity is now allowed, as we know trees of true reality, nourish the balance.
Dark Coal for the light, to illuminate a path to new paradigms.

There are plenty of blankets in these woods, made of comfort and hope.
If only for a while, it's better than none.

One for all, all for one, even if your forest of anguish is overgrown.

Ones of Angels, Some of Demons

We see evil faces, their mug shots look the same, dark crevasses for eyes,
Soul black as a universal void, they all mingle, now dispersing to hide.

Humans of love and care, project smiles when they are sullen,
Or down, their true nature flutters from their eyes.

Smiles pulled tight, puckered evil lips; the evil exudes from their jaws.
How much innocence have they consumed?

Positivity radiates from the wrinkles of a kind face, an energy to behold,
Infectious portrait pictures tell a tale of love for all.

We see demons on the TV, a shadow cloaks their face, they lie and lie,
We spot from miles away, all the way to private islands.

A face of truthfulness, care, and compassion, becomes engulfed in light,
One man stands out, he is from a small Caribbean island.

The profile, of one tells a million and one stories, ones of love and devotion,
While others leave you with that horrible, gut feeling.

The face, a gateway to witness a souls true meaning.

Unexpected Protector

The raven black of night cloaked with omens of oblivion, why do we judge,
It protected energy in a vessel of skin.
The entities that take the light of the innocent, the raven makes its descent,
Reveals himself to repent the sin.
The eye of the bird, onyx, as it casts the shadow on souls that need to be consumed,
To protect the fallen from the grim.
Alas the bird reveals his angel, tearing away the wings to present to the falling,

A gift to help them protect and fly on a whim.

Recycling Champions

The child with no food always shares.
Smiles around people with good intentions.
Releasing karma through suffering while surviving.
The man with no legs walks many roads,
With clarity, clear perspective, vigor, and hope.
The man with all four limbs drags himself down only
one.
The abused remain strong, strengthening with each
day,
Awesome outlook of life, while the comfortable melt,
Over the material world.
Trauma Victims will hide, eventually they break
through,
blackened blankets to shine through, their light
illuminates the world.
Suffering ignites fires, strengthening the soul.
Be thoughtful, be mindful, be thankful for those living
the opposite life.
So majorities can be at ease, and the universe will not
stand still.
True compassion will lead us all through.
When you think the world is against you,
Think of all above.

When it Counts

De Wolf, the beast, swimming in a coat of red arms,
the second richest man in an American.

Made millions from slavery, suspiciously the family tree has gone.

My brothers and sisters of colour, I feel your pain, I see the horror of the past, and present.
A show still being played out by the puppeteers.

We need to stick together, rigid and controlled, an unbreakable bond from the bottom.
While we are divided by pettiness, achievability will be none.

Being oppressed as we are, being poisoned by mental health and fear.
We are banging in a soundproof box, smash it, and true justice will appear.

Slavers haven't gone, Chameleons only change their tone, they've got us dancing to a new tune.
Sex and materialism, our eyes closed, staring down the barrel of a gun.

The sheer number of the persecuted together, would cause a tidal wave of true meaning.
The powers that be would cut their losses and run, screaming.

Governments are puppets and armor for those that run the show, we need to push past them,
Drop petty differences and be mindful, we strive for the same goal.

Until the above is achieved, I sit here in peace,
shouting in gags of society, will only cause more pain.
When a rebellion starts, give me a shout.

Chapter Four:
ALL ELSE

Way of the Witcher

The entity with eyes of gold, powers that shifts molds,
Toss the Witcher a coin, a service of blood to behold.
Word in Oxenfurt, they are heartless, Triss, and Yennefer
decline.
They have seen through the Axii, mind control where he can
hide.
Creatures who enter his heart, forced to break down the walls,
Like Nograd, impregnable, scholars say they will never fall.
They call him butcher of Blaviken, a battle he did not wish,
Majorities curse at Geralt, no rest for this....
Cries for help erupt, when Alghouls are roaming, Gryphons in
the nest.
Population now hailing the demon, the best, the best, the best.
His heart beats truly for she so powerful, Ciri is the one.
Through the Witcher's existence, never understood.
Now all is done, he rides into the sun, who follows beside?
It's dandelion... Roach galloped, they left him behind!

Tangible Game of Thrones

Possibly upon us, a new world order, a sunflower blossoming
to show the inner,
It stretches back to old laws, the ones at the pinnacle, they
abide and die by.

Illegitimate the case put forward; an entity awaits in shadow,
seeds lay dormant,

Palaces sleep empty with renovation, splitting organisations, turmoil and retribution.

Out of one's mind while planets align, while events on track, meandering as time.
The line stops before full circle, presented to us, an oxbow lake, a mark in history.

Games of thrones are played, battles between roses are maintained,
To most these affairs are a whimsical story, born from yesterday's mysteries.

The lands have been softened for new roots to grow, for a base of establishment.
The blood of the Pearl falcon may evaporate and rise, possibly causing rain.

The make up of most stories, is a mixology of truths, lies and tales,
This is a beautiful time in the inevitable history to see how this chapter unfolds.

Headdresses exchange as flames extinguish,
New flames before your eyes.

Horology

Thomas Mudge, the creator, the thinker of the bracelet on a wrist, a time piece,
To keep track of life's appointments and the suns position.
Thomas was more than a watchmaker, he was a horologist, time keeping was not his design.
He created a piece of the cosmos, never ending movement, sublime.

Was Mudge reading and studying, or meditating on life, how
our cells never stop.
The energy is perpetual, it never ends, like the calendar of the
watch.
The high price tag is not for the brand, but a slither of a great
understanding and mind.
The meticulous design, specs of screws, the balance of a
halfmoon, a galaxy at hand.
Humans and Society are no different from a watch, that is
why we are breaking down.
Modern life is like a battery watch, a struggle to keep going
around.

Varvara

A Swedish Beauty was mine, never belonged to me, she was
free.
From the front, her contours of bliss excited me.
From the rear, her large trunk, wow, oh my.
Her purr begins to break, more money she takes.
I leave her behind and move on.

Now from Tokyo with love, so divine, her shape stole my
mind.
Her intelligence amazed, as I gazed over her exterior,
My heart desired the ride.
Jealousy attempted to hurt her, but her skin was hard as a
dragon's,
Her premature death, came from lack of attention.

Finally, I met her, the American, world ties, a little rough on
the eye.
An older lady, had taken care of herself on the inside.
Well-travelled but kept her miles low, true wisdom.

I'll cherish her forever, take care of all her needs, I question my judgment?

I should have had, an old Ford from the start!

You're Staying

Demon, oh demon, you found me, crawled into my vessel as a child.
You mocked me and plagued my thoughts for decades.
Evil spirit, you danced and trampled my heart, like the African plains, dry, it burnt.
The stampede of a million wildebeest, the hurt.
You hoodwinked me, into thinking kindness meant violence, my main spirit, incoherent.
Axes and bullets rain down, my psyche bolts awake.
Demon, oh demon, you really fucked up now, you're crawling away, I think not.
You're staying put, you will sit in peace and watch.
I'll drag you back, now you can suffer in my love, until my days are done.

About The Author

Ellis Robinson

https://www.unchainedwisdom.com/

https://www.facebook.com/ellis.unchained.1

https://twitter.com/unchainedwisdom?lang=en

Work of Unchained Wisdom ©2020

Printed in Great Britain
by Amazon

59610959R00037